Choose Truth

tiny wonder
PUBLISHING

Choose Truth

A 6-Week Journey to Becoming a God-Confident Daughter

by Jamie Klusacek
with Hannah Grieser

Choose Truth

Copyright © 2024 by Jamie Klusacek

All rights reserved. No part of this book may be used or reproduced in any manner whatsoever without written permission except in the case of brief quotations embodied in critical articles and reviews.

First published in the United States by Tiny Wonder Publishing
First Printing, 2024

ISBN: 978-1-7361181-6-0 Paperback
Library of Congress Control Number: 2023923256

Cover and Interior Design: Milan Klusacek
Cover Photo: Roman Odintsov

"This I know, that God is for me."

Psalm 56:9, Amplified Bible

HOW TO USE THIS BOOK

This book is a 6-week journey to becoming a God-confident daughter.

Each week, we'll focus on a lie that we may be believing about ourselves—then we will dive into the truth of who God says we are according to His Word. The weeks are made up of five daily readings based on a Bible verse, followed by a daily prayer to help you build the habit of listening and talking to God.

There are also little spots for you to take notes. Have fun! Get some new highlighters. Write in the margins. Scribble down what God is speaking about who you REALLY are in Him, based on His Word. Underline things that stick out to you. Enjoy the journey.

Sprinkled throughout, you'll also find quotes from God-confident women. Feel free to follow them on their social channels if you're on social media. I encourage you to start surrounding yourself with the right women—women who speak God's Truth and will help breathe God-confidence into your heart.

Preface

YOU have been on my heart for a long time, beautiful girl.

I wish at this moment that we could be face to face. I'd sit you on my cherry red Pottery Barn sofa. Wrap you up in my softest blanket and give you one of those big motherly hugs. You know the ones: where your mom hugs you so long she seems to take all your cares and worries away with her. I'd make you a hot cup of tea and serve you freshly baked chocolate chip cookies. We would eat, laugh, share stories, and just be together.

Listening to you talk openly and honestly, my love for you would only grow stronger. And I would be certain of a few things about your life. First, whether you see it or not, you have a desire for God. You might already know this, but if you don't, then let me tell you: it's there. Secondly, I would know that our paths crossing was no accident; it was a divine act of God and His desires for you.

Sweet Daughter, even here and now as you're reading this, it is no accident. God is coming after you. He's pursuing you with all the love in His heart.

You might wonder, does God even care about me? Does He even hear the secret prayers I've been praying for months or years? Does He see the desires of MY heart? The answer to all those questions is yes. He hears you. He sees you. He loves you. And this book in your hands is part of His answer to your prayers.

So as you read, I pray that you are reminded of the promises of God for YOUR life. I pray that you exchange your faulty truth for His life-giving Truth. And I pray that as you release the lies you believe about yourself, you will find a fresh, heavenly perspective that only YOUR Father in heaven can give.

You are loved just as you are. You are worthy just as you are. Your life has a great purpose. You are cherished. You are beautiful. God loves you and He's surrounding you with people who love you too.

A mama in the faith,

Jamie

Jamie Kay Klusacek
Author

Table of Contents

14	Foreword
16	Week 1: Value
38	Week 2: Identity
62	Week 3: Performance
84	Week 4: Purpose
106	Week 5: Relationships
128	Week 6: Truth
155	Salvation Prayer
156	About the Authors
161	Acknowledgments
163	Photography
164	Footnotes

Foreword

In 2016, THERE{4} Gathering was born with a singular purpose: to have a lasting impact on the next generation of teen girls. Since then, we have witnessed the incredible transformation of thousands of girls at our live conferences and countless more around the world through livestream views. Our ministry has flourished with the combination of exceptional teachers, dynamic worship, and a community of amazing girls. However, at the core of everything we do lies the unshakable foundation of God's Word.

This devotional, which you now hold in your hands, is more than just a book. It is a roadmap designed to guide you on your journey of walking with and towards Jesus in every aspect of your life. While it does not seek to replace the Bible, it serves as a friendly mentor to lead you deeper into the heart of Jesus through His Word.

Within these pages, you will find daily reflections and thought-provoking insights that encourage spiritual growth. Each entry beckons you to spend intentional time with God, allowing His truth to permeate your heart and mind. As you devote yourself to this devotional, may the words inspire and challenge you to embrace a life lived for Jesus.

We are honored to walk alongside you in this journey of faith. Our hope is that you will use this devotional not merely as a guide, but as a constant reminder of the transforming power of God's Word. May it encourage you, strengthen you, and equip you to impact the world around you. Let's embark on this adventure together as we let God's truth shape our lives, illuminate our path, and compel us to live out His purposes each day.

With love and anticipation for the great things God will do through you,

Tiffany Daniels
Founder and Visionary, THERE{4} Gathering

WEEK ONE

Let's talk about your *value*

Week One
Let's talk about your value

I'M NOT WORTHY OF LOVE.

TRUTH

I AM VALUABLE IN THE EYES OF GOD.

I am accepted and deeply loved. I am His child. Before I lift a finger, I am fiercely loved and valued by Him and nothing I do will ever change that.

Day One

"This is my dearly loved Son, who brings me great joy."

(Matthew 3:17, NLT)

We are starting this week by combating the lie that you are unloved. In fact, that specific lie couldn't be further from the truth. You are deeply loved by your heavenly Father.

I love this passage in Matthew 3, the first book in the New Testament. Before Jesus ever does anything worthwhile in the eyes of others, God speaks in an audible voice from heaven and says the words in the verse above to Jesus. The same words He spoke over Jesus He speaks over you, His daughter.

God calls YOU His daughter. The word "Son" in this passage means offspring, legitimate descendant, one who God cherishes, to view with favor, to desire, to choose with pleasure. When God calls you beloved daughter, it's as if He's saying to you: Baby girl, you are my daughter. I have marked you not only with My love, but with My identity. I know your true value and worth. With your identity as My child comes the love, care, provision, power, and authority that only I can bestow. You are Mine.

The word "loved" in this passage means being the object of a peculiar love, a holy bond, to be dear. You are loved by God. This very minute, He is thinking about you and loving you. His love is not based on what you have done or haven't done. It's not based on whether you have good grades or have utterly failed every class. It's not based on what others think about you or how you view God. It's not determined on how you look or feel. He simply, purely loves you.

And that's not the end of this beautiful promise for your life. God tops it all off by saying "you bring Me great joy." Joy is different from tolerance. It is far different from mindless acceptance. Sometimes I think we believe God is simply tolerant of us, treating us like that awkward classmate we're forced to sit next to in science class. That is not the way God views you or your life. He takes joy and pleasure in you. He wants to be with you. In fact, He would choose to be with you a thousand times over.

So next time you are tempted to view yourself as less than what God intended, I want you to repeat to yourself, "I am a joy to God." What God was saying to Jesus, He is saying to you today: You are my gorgeous daughter. You are fabulously loved. And I'm over the moon about you.

Prayer

God, today I start out my week by thanking You that I am loved. You take great joy in being with me, in being my Father. Help me see my life the way You see my life today.

Bring it *home*

How does being loved by God change my view of myself?

_____
_____
_____
_____
_____
_____

Before I lift a finger, I am *fiercely loved* and *valued by God* and nothing I do will ever change that.

—Jamie Klusacek

Day Two

" See how very much our Father loves us, for he calls us his children, and that is what we are!"

(I John 3:1, NLT)

Let's talk about love. Many times when we think of the word "love," we think of a feeling or an emotion. In our culture, it seems easy to fall out of love with someone else. Many of you have probably experienced divorce in your family or watched your friends go through a family split. You may have seen couples who appear to be hopelessly in love one minute and in the middle of a breakup the next. We can't help but wonder: what is love, and what keeps it alive?

From the outside, it appears that love is dependent on our feelings and maybe even on our performance. If we can just be good enough, that person will never leave us. If we try to figure out what that friend likes, maybe we can adjust our character to be what they want.

Let's face it: the way we see love modeled in the world around us can be confusing, unappealing, exhausting, and at times hurtful. So it's important from the beginning of our studies in God's Word that we understand what kind of love God has towards us.

The word "love" in this verse is referring to a type of love called agape love. It's the highest, most pure love we could ever experience. Agape love is someone choosing to love you whether they feel like it or not. It's a love that serves others with humility. It embodies kindness and devotion. It is not motivated by emotions, good feelings, attraction, or things you have or haven't done in order for the person to love you. In fact, you could epically fail and agape love will still love you like crazy. It's unwavering.

And not only does God love you with this type of love—but agape love is literally who God is. In the Bible, John says that God is love, agape love (1 John 4:16). He can't act in any other love towards you because it would be against His character. He loves you deeply, and that will NEVER change.

So next time the lie that you are unloved comes knocking at your door—wanting to get into your house, sit in your chair, and eat all your favorite snacks in the pantry—just shut the front door in its face. Don't allow that lie to steal one second of your time.

Remind yourself today how loved you are by God.

Prayer

Father, thank You for deeply loving me as Your child. It's not the kind of love that will disappoint in the end; it's a sure, steadfast love that will stand the test of time. Thank You for loving me in my past, present, and future.

Bring it *home*

How is God's agape love different from love I've experienced?

_____

_____

_____

_____

God doesn't love us *because* of our worth,

We are of worth *because* God loves us.

– Martin Luther

Day Three

"I have inscribed you on the palms of My hands; Your walls are continually before Me."

(Isaiah 49:16, NKJV)

There's a reason why you don't see tattoos on the palms of people's hands. First of all, it would be four times more sensitive to get a tattoo on your palm than on your shoulder or calf. So, to get a tattoo there seems crazy. And secondly, you could never cover it up—that is, unless you decided to wear winter gloves all year round, even in the summertime. So why does God use the analogy of "inscribing us on the palms of His hands" to show us how much He loves His children?

He's trying to make a point. In this passage, God is talking to the children of Israel in the Old Testament. Being in captivity caused them to wonder if God had forgotten about them. They had serious questions about God and doubted that He really cared for them. God answered their concerns through Isaiah by saying the verse above. The same truths apply to us today as God's children. God wants you to know how loved you are and that He is thinking about you all the time. The same love God has for His children in the Old Testament, He has for you!

Think about it: we use our hands for everything! Brushing our teeth, combing our hair, putting on our makeup, driving our car, doing schoolwork, scrolling on our phones, eating, drinking—almost everything besides sleeping! So imagine if you had a tattoo on your palm. It wouldn't be something you could easily forget or cover up. And that's another point He's making: God hasn't forgotten about you. You may wonder if God really does care and if He has your best interest at heart in relation to His will. My sweet, beautifully loved daughter, He does!

The second part of this passage refers to walls. What kind of promise do walls give us about God's love for us? In this story, "walls" refer specifically to the walls of Jerusalem and figuratively to God's people. In Isaiah's time, walls spoke of strength, health, prosperity, and security in God. That's a lot of promise found in walls. But the promise stands true for us today.

God is always mindful of you and your walls! He cares about your strength, your health, your security, and your provision in life—and you know what? It's all found through Him. Even when we find ourselves doubting God, His love stands immovable for us.

Prayer

God, thank You for Your love and thank You for the promises found in Your Word! I stand on the promise today that I am not forgotten, but deeply, immovably loved by You. Thank You for having my best interest at heart.

Bring it *home*

How does being known by God impact my relationship with Him?

_____

_____

_____

_____

"There is no fear in love, but perfect love casts out fear. For fear has to do with punishment, and whoever fears has not been perfected in love." —1 John 4.18, ESV

The secret to joy is to keep seeking God where we doubt He is.

-Ann Voskamp

Day *Four*

"There is no fear in love, but perfect love casts out fear. For fear has to do with punishment, and whoever fears has not been perfected in love."

1 JOHN 4:18, ESV

I highly encourage you to take a few minutes to read all of 1 John. It's only five chapters and it is near the end of your Bible.

Being unlovable starts out as a lie in our minds. If we believe the lie for too long, it can turn into fear: fear of not being loved or of disappointing people, which isn't a fun way to live. The good news is, once we truly take hold of God's truth—that we are loved by God with agape love—we will stop being motivated by lies or fear and rest assured in the love of our Father.

The word "perfect" in the verse above means more than just knowing about the agape love of God. It means that God's love has actually accomplished its goal or purpose in you. God's love is made perfect when you know, understand, embrace, accept, and live fully in His love. And living in God's perfect love means that you are complete—you don't need anyone or anything else to fill a void in your life. You lack nothing. That sounds like a peaceful place to live, wouldn't you agree?

You see, when we allow God's love to be perfected in us, there's a promise attached to it: God's perfect love casts out all fear. And the Bible doesn't mean it just tosses fear gently to the curb; it literally means that God's perfect love will violently throw out all fear in your life. This is the kind of fear that causes us to doubt God's love for us. It's the kind of fear that makes us tremble at the lies swirling around us. It's the kind of fear that doubts God's goodness in our lives. It robs us of hope and steals our joy in the present because we are constantly worrying about the future. It causes us to push harder for people to like us instead of resting in the love God has already gifted us. All that fear has no place in our lives when we fully embrace God's love for us.

And of course, we can't fully understand or accept this kind of love on our own, but we can ask for the help of the Holy Spirit who lives inside of us. In John 14:16, Jesus says that the Holy Spirit is our Helper. I don't know about you, but I need all the help I can get to have God's agape love perfected in me.

Let's make a commitment before God and each other to allow God's perfect love to fill every area of our lives from here on out.

Prayer

Father, I need Your help so that Your perfect love takes root in my heart, mind, soul, spirit—really, in every part of me. Would You help me to be transformed by Your love and to rest securely in You? Would You kick every fear out of my life—today, tomorrow, and forever!

Bring it *home*

If perfect love casts out all fear, where in my life am I afraid? And where do I need to trust in God's love?

_____
_____
_____
_____
_____

We have to start with the character of God.

Everything has been made *through Him* and *for Him.*

We see who we are through Him.

—Ruth Chou Simons

Day *Five*

"For You formed my inward parts; You covered me in my mother's womb. I will praise You, for I am fearfully and wonderfully made."

Psalm 139 is one of those chapters that you want to print out, hang on your mirror, and read frequently throughout your day. It oozes with God's love and care for His children. Many times we talk about the love that our mother had for us, carrying us inside her belly for nine months, but God's love surpasses that. He took the time to form us in our mother's womb.

When the Bible uses the word "womb," it implies God's sovereign care, comfort, and calling on your life even before you were born. God was thinking about you even before you were born! So if you are ever tempted to think that God doesn't love you, reading about the intricate way He formed you before you were born should silence that lie.

Let's talk about these words: care, comfort, and calling.

CARE: God cared for you then, and He cares for you now. He cares about your hopes, your dreams, and your disappointments. He cares about that thing at school that is frustrating you and that friend who's left you unopened on Snap. He cares about every detail of your life, so bring it all to Him in prayer. Talk out loud to Him when no one is around. Let His care lead you to open, honest conversations with Him.

COMFORT: God is ready and willing to comfort you, and He is comforting you now. Do you ever just need a shoulder to cry on? Someone to hug you tight and take away some of the things you are carrying? Well, God is there for that too! The word "comfort" means to reassure and to bring cheer to someone. God wants to be your comfort throughout life, so let Him. He loves you enough to help carry your disappointments and setbacks.

CALLING: God called you before you were born, and you are still called. No matter what the world tells you, no matter what lies scream at you—you are called by God to love Him and share Him with the world around you. With Him, He calls you: strong (2 Corinthians 12:10), victorious (1 John 5:4), courageous (Joshua 1:9) and never alone (Isaiah 41:10).

Remember these promises on the road ahead, and above all else remember how deeply loved you are.

Prayer

God, I thank You for teaching me about Your love for me and who I am in You. I thank You today for Your care, Your comfort, and Your calling that has rested on my life even before I was born. I choose to embrace Your love. Help me to love You too.

Bring it *home*

Talk through being cared for, comforted by, and called by God. What do those words mean to you?

_____

_____

_____

_____

WEEK TWO

Let's talk about your *identity*

Week *Two*
Let's talk about your identity

(LIE)

MY IDENTITY IS FOUND IN MY SUCCESSES & FAILURES.

(TRUTH)

MY IDENTITY IS FOUND IN GOD.

My identity is not found in what I do; it's found in God. I am a child of God. I will let God alone form my identity.

Day One

"If we claim we have no sin, we are only fooling ourselves and not living in the truth. But if we confess our sins to him, he is faithful and just to forgive us our sins."

I John 1:8-9, NLT

Let's just set this straight from the beginning of our week: Our identity is not based on our successes or failures. To live like we will never fail or as if we have no weakness is actually living in denial of being human!

When we fail (and we all will), let's not say things like "I AM a failure." Because that is not the truth. The truth is "What I did failed." It's: I made a poor choice. I did something that I knew I shouldn't. I spoke behind my friend's back, and that was wrong. I was really mean to my parents. I made a mistake with that guy, and I feel terrible. I didn't excel at something I tried. Remind yourself: What I did may have failed, but who I am remains constant. I am still a deeply loved child of God. I am already right in God's sight because of what Jesus did for me on the cross. Period.

The beautiful thing is that God can use our moments of failure to mold and shape us to be more like Him. Through the help of the Holy Spirit, we can be transformed from the inside out. This doesn't mean we will ever be perfect; in and of ourselves, we never will. But if we bring those failures to God, confess our sin, and ask Him to shape us, we can learn to see failures as a blessing instead of something to be ashamed of.

Failures, when brought to God, can open our eyes to see how much we need God in our lives. God doesn't want our failures to change our identity; only He deserves the right to shape and define who we are. As we bring our failures to Him, He can mature us. Nothing is wasted in God's plan. Who knows? Maybe that failure will be something that God will use in the future to help bring others closer to Him.

It's time for us to lay the shame down, pick up the gracious gift of God, and start moving forward in freedom. Trust that God will help you make wise choices in the future and learn from the past in the process.

Prayer

God, I trust You with not only my victories but my failures too. Only You deserve the right to define who I am. I thank You that nothing I could ever do will change how You view me. When I mess up, fail, or sin, help me be quick to repent, come to You, and see myself the way You do.

Bring it *home*

Where in my life am I allowing failure to define my worth?

_____

_____

_____

_____

_____

I AM WHO GOD SAYS I AM.

Day Two

"And we know that God causes everything to work together for the good of those who love God and are called according to his purpose for them."

Romans 8:28, NLT

Here's a promise for us to stand on today. Releasing what we've done wrong and embracing our identity in God comes through trusting God, grabbing ahold of His Word, and surrendering to Him in all we do. In that process, He helps us exchange our thoughts with His thoughts of us.

God promises that He will cause EVERYTHING to work together for good for those who love Him. He doesn't say SOME things. He doesn't say: "Everything that's not a really big mistake in your life will work together for good." He says ALL things. This means the good, the bad, the ugly—all things will work together for good in your life when you love Him.

The word "good" implies that good will happen whether we see it or not. Here's where trusting in God's Word is so important. Your situation might not look good right now. You may have epically failed (we all do), but trust that God will use it for a good purpose in the future as you follow Him. Goodness also means that God will give us the power we need to walk with faith in Him and make the right choices.

This promise is for those who love God and are called according to His purpose. The word "love" here means that we embrace God's will for our lives and obey Him through His power. It's a choice that we have to honor Him above our own preference, thoughts, or feelings. This is God's invitation for you, His daughter, to believe and receive the gift of salvation through Jesus.

Not only does God invite us to receive His salvation—not by any merit of our own, but because we are given the power to believe and love God—but on top of that, God promises to work all things together for good in our lives.

May this promise fuel you in your identity as you move forward. As you love God with your whole heart, rest in the fact that He is working behind the scenes for your good.

Prayer

Father, I trust that You have the power to work all things together for good in my life. Thank You that it's not by my strength that I need to accomplish this—but it's all through You. I love You.

Bring it *home*

What do I need God to turn around for good in my life?

_____
_____
_____
_____
_____
_____
_____

We don't need more
more

achieving *and* attaining

making *and* dividing

hustling *and* distraction

We just need more of

Jesus.

Then everything would be less about us!
-Charlotte Gambill

Day Three

"The Lord was with Joseph, so he succeeded in everything he did as he served in the home of his Egyptian master."

Genesis 39:2, NLT

We are learning to embrace God's Word and trust that even in our huge mess-ups, He can work it together for good. But what about our ultimate successes in life? Where do those fit into our understanding of who we are and who God is?

Let's go to the story of an amazing person in the Bible, a man named Joseph. Joseph was one of 12 brothers, but brotherhood wasn't all it was cracked up to be in Joseph's family. You see, his father loved Joseph more than any of the other brothers, and he made it really obvious. He gave Joseph a special brilliantly colored coat to wear. It was like Joseph was wearing a neon sign that said, "Remember everyone, I am the most loved child." Well, that didn't sit very well with his other brothers, so they decided to sell their brother into slavery and lie to their father about it. They told their dad that Joseph was killed by a wild animal.

Ok. Let's stop here. If you thought you had bad family dynamics, think again. It probably doesn't include siblings selling each other and pretending like you died—and if it does, know that Joseph can relate.

The cool thing about this story is that even though the unimaginable happened to Joseph, God was with him. You see, Joseph loved God and the Bible says that wherever he went and whatever he did, God made Joseph prosper. Even in the house he was sold into as a slave, God made him succeed. It didn't matter if it was in his home as a son, serving as a slave, in prison, or eventually the palace—as Joseph loved and honored God, God honored him in the eyes of those around him.

The same is true for you, Daughter. When it comes to success, it doesn't matter where you find yourself or what season you're in—as you love God, He will bless you in His special way, even in the hardships. He can make you succeed and thrive in even the direst of circumstances. In those moments, remember: success does not happen because we are better than anyone else, it is all a gift from God. It's His power that helps us to overcome.

Next time you ace that test, get promoted to captain of the team, demonstrate patience, or have the courage to tackle a hard situation, take time out to thank God for giving you all that you needed. Remember, whether you're the captain or a permanent bench warmer—you are deeply loved and valued by God.

Prayer

God, I thank You that You are in my failures and successes. Thank You for giving me the strength, wisdom, and talent to grow and experience Your blessing in my life as I place You first.

Bring it *home*

In what areas of my life can I give God the credit for success?

God, I trust You with not only my victories, but my failures too. Only You deserve the right to define who I am. I thank You that nothing I could ever do will change how You view me. When I mess up, fail, or sin, help me be quick to repent, come to You, and see myself the way you do.

If we're not *careful,* our whole identity can be wrapped up in what *other people think* we're supposed to be or *what we think* we're supposed to do.

-Jamie Ivey

Day *Four*

"The fear of the Lord is the beginning of knowledge..."

Proverbs 1:7, NKJV

Now, before you say something like, "I knew it! I should be afraid of God. Even the Bible says that I should fear God"—let's take a step back and talk about what it really means to fear God.

First of all, this isn't the type of fear that we experience when watching that horror film we know we shouldn't be watching. It's not the type of fear that causes us to be paralyzed in our steps and tremble in fright. This type of fear is a positive quality. It's a reverence that acknowledges God's perfect and holy character. It's the type of fear that moves us towards honoring God. To revere God means that you choose to honor Him above anything else in your life. It's the beginning of you having a proper view of who God is and who you are.

You see, you give power to the thing that you fear the most. Because you revere and value it, you allow it to influence your life. And it begins to shape how you respond. Think of this: if you fear being average, you'll work extra hard to succeed in what's placed before you. If you fear the boogeyman, you probably won't go into your basement at night. If you fear being unhealthy or overweight, you might not celebrate by eating cake with that loved one. If you fear poverty, you'll pursue wealth. If you fear being friendless and alone, you'll probably do all you can not to offend people and try to be everything for everybody. Fear can be fuel for your life—but only the fear of God actually produces wisdom for your journey.

If you fear failure or success above your fear and reverence of God, it will leave you stuck in life. You won't want to believe God for too much because you'll fear that you will fail. You won't step into that new opportunity because you don't think you have what it takes.

The thing is, beautiful daughter, when we choose to fear God above all else, our failures lose their hold on us. We can walk confidently on the road ahead because we know Who we belong to and that nothing we could ever do will change God's love for us.

The good, holy, reverent fear of God coupled with humility leads to our fullest life!

Prayer

Father, help me to fear You above everything else in my life. Not in a scary way, but in a way that I place You before it all. Sometimes this is hard for me, but teach me to choose You even when I don't feel like it. I love You.

Bring it *home*

Do I struggle with the fear of failure? Why or why not?

_____

_____

_____

_____

_____

No one has
the *power*
to define you

other
than

the ONE
who created you.

—Hosanna Wong

Day *Five*

"Faith shows the reality of what we hope for; it is the evidence of things we cannot see ... It is impossible to please God without faith. Anyone who wants to come to him must believe that God exists and that he rewards those who sincerely seek him."

Hebrews 11:1 & 6, NLT

I want to help grow your faith today. When we carry the weight of our successes or failures on our shoulders, it's like a bucket of water tossed over an open fire. It can dim our faith in God. But faith, sweet Daughter, is what fuels our trusting relationship with God. It is a quality that pleases God. Faith is trusting not only in what Jesus did for the world by dying on the cross for our sins, but believing that God still has the power to change our lives from the inside out today.

So what do you need faith for today? Remember faith isn't something that you can just accomplish on your own. It's believing that Someone greater than yourself has the power to change your life—specifically, God. Let's throw the applause of success out the window. Let's toss the shame of failure in the trash. And let's just commit to believe in God.

I'm sure many of you have heard of the fruits of the Spirit in Galatians 5. They are: love, joy, peace, patience, kindness, goodness, gentleness, faithfulness, and self-control. When you surrender your life to Jesus, these are qualities He wants to develop in you through the power of the Holy Spirit.

This word "faithfulness" here doesn't mean that you are going to be unwaveringly committed to people in your life. It doesn't mean you will never miss a game, practice, or rehearsal at school—it's not that type of faithfulness. In this passage, it means to be faith-filled. It means that God will give you the ability to believe Him in faith all the days of your life. You will stay full of faith for your past. You will stay drenched in faith for your present. And you will be confidently full of faith in God for the future ahead.

Remember, even if you can't see everything that God is doing with your eyes, trust that He has your best interest at heart. Faith doesn't mean we will understand everything. Faith implies that even though we can't see it, we can choose to trust God.

Let's decide that we will live our life full of faith in God.

Prayer

God, help me to stay faith-filled for You. Not filled up with faith in myself or what I can or cannot do, but filled up with faith in You. Thank You, Father.

Bring it *home*

Where in my life can I start believing God in faith?

_____

_____

_____

_____

_____

WEEK THREE

Let's talk about your *performance*

Week *Three*
Let's talk about your performance

(LIE)

I MUST BE PERFECT IN ORDER TO BE A REAL CHRISTIAN.

TRUTH

NO ONE IS PERFECT EXCEPT GOD.

Everyone has sinned and falls short of God's standard. No one is perfect except God alone.

Day One

"For everyone has sinned; we all fall short of God's glorious standard. Yet God, in his grace, freely makes us right in his sight. He did this through Christ Jesus when he freed us from the penalty for our sins."

Romans 3:23-24, NLT

God doesn't need you to be perfect. He wants your presence, not your perfection. So, how do you view yourself? Is your view of yourself keeping you from a really great friendship with God?

When you look in the mirror or evaluate your day, what thoughts run through your mind? It would be awesome if your thoughts were 100% positive, but that is probably not the case. We live in a world that promotes perfection—or at least a perfect image. It's estimated that one in four people deal with perfectionism, meaning they have abnormally high personal standards and critical self-evaluations. Perfectionism makes it feel like life is an endless test that constantly picks apart our achievements and looks.

When we view life through the lens of being perfect, it's easy to think that God holds us to the same impossible standards. We secretly think that if we aren't perfect, we can't have a deep, lasting relationship with God. Daughter, this could not be further from the truth.

One of the biggest mindsets that creates a wedge between us and God is thinking that we have to be perfect before we can come to Him. Perfectionism makes us feel like we have to hide from God and isolate ourselves from others when we miss the mark. It's the oldest trick in the book. When Adam and Eve committed the first sin in Genesis 3, they "felt shame," covered themselves in fig leaves, and "hid from God among the trees."

You don't have to hide. God doesn't want your perfection; He wants your presence. Jesus lived a perfect life so that we don't have to. Because Jesus died on the cross for your sins, you have constant access to God.

He sees you through the lens of Jesus–perfection. You are right in His sight.

Prayer

God, thank You that I don't have to wait until I'm perfect to have a relationship with You. You take me as I am and lavish Your love on me! Will You forgive me for the times when I rejected Your love because I felt like I didn't deserve it? Today, I accept the grace of Jesus that makes me perfect in Your sight—not because of what I do, but because of what Jesus already did.

Bring it *home*

Do I try to hide from God when I mess up? Why?

_____

_____

_____

_____

_____

perfectly *messy*

In a world that says we have to be perfect to be used, God is saying He'll use us right in the middle of our *mess.*

— *Toni Collier*

Day Two

"But he said to me, 'My grace is sufficient for you, for my power is made perfect in weakness.' Therefore I will boast all the more gladly of my weaknesses, so that the power of Christ may rest upon me."

2 Corinthians 12:9, ESV

God doesn't expect you to be perfect. And what if He actually prefers your imperfection? The real you, in all of your authentic, raw, and broken beauty.

Now, of course God doesn't want you to stay in a cycle of sin. He does, however, want you to be honest with Him about the struggle. God wants a relationship with you, not simply religion and rituals. The goal is not to "figure it out" on your own and try to become perfect in your own strength. Rather, God wants to walk alongside you in your imperfection and help you walk in faith as you let Him transform your life.

When we try to be perfect, we limit God's infinite power by choosing to exhaust our limited power. However, when we invite God into our imperfection, we exchange our weakness for His strength and allow Him to get the glory instead of ourselves.

That's exactly what the Apostle Paul talks about in 2 Corinthians 12:9. Earlier in this same chapter, we learn that Paul had a "thorn in his flesh" that he begged God to take away. God's response was always the same: "My grace is sufficient for you, for my power is made perfect in weakness." Wow. Paul had a "thorn"—an imperfection, a painful struggle—and God did not take it away or tell him to try harder. Instead, God encouraged Paul to lean into His grace.

Similarly, we can't see and accept the sufficiency of God's grace until we make peace with our own insufficiency. If we didn't have weaknesses, we would not need God. Often, God lets our weaknesses remain so that we remember to depend on Him. This isn't because God's a control freak; it's because He loves us. If we were completely self-sufficient, we'd miss out on a wonderful relationship and partnership with our Creator. We would try to become our own god.

When you invite God into your imperfections and weaknesses, His power will start working in those areas. You will have powerful testimonies about how God healed, comforted, redeemed, strengthened, and used the broken places in your life. As Paul said, "For when I am weak, I am strong." That's a truth that will shatter the lies of perfectionism time and time again!

Prayer

God, thank You for Your grace! I want to know what it's like to have Your power work in my weakness. Will You show me? Please free me from any shame I have about my imperfections. I trust You to redeem the broken parts of my story, heal the wounds from my past, and make me strong in my weaknesses.

Bring it *home*

What weaknesses in my life do I need to give God?

_____

_____

_____

breathe in
His grace

When we hide the mess we've been through, we also hide the redemption that God has lavishly poured on us. We can't proclaim His grace until we expose our mess.

-Jamie Ivey

Day Three

"The thief comes only to steal and kill and destroy. I came that they may have life and have it abundantly."

John 10:10, ESV

It's 5:30 a.m. on a Monday and your alarm starts to blare. You hit snooze more than a few times and scramble out of bed to get ready. As you eat breakfast, you scroll through social media. At school, you see hundreds of other girls with perfect makeup and the latest fashion trends. At practice, you compare your athletic ability to your teammates. After a long day, you finally get home surrounded by piles of homework and parents with high academic expectations of you. It's exhausting.

In our success-driven, social-media-filled culture, we are surrounded by a multitude of voices suggesting how we should live our lives. Every day, we make thousands of decisions—35,000 to be exact![1] If we're not careful, we can spend all our energy trying to keep up. Before we know it, we're trying to meet a million expectations and we don't know which ones we even truly care about.

Our focus can shift to what we are missing rather than what we have. We start viewing life through the lens of lack, but God invites us to view life from a lens of abundance.

Jesus said, "The thief comes only to steal and kill and destroy. I came that they may have life and have it abundantly." One of the main ways the enemy will try to steal from you is through how you see yourself. He wants you to think that you will never be enough or have enough, which will leave you in a stressful state of striving for perfection.

Here's the truth: in a world of endless expectations, you have everything you need for today. Instead of focusing on how far you have to go, focus on what you've been given. Instead of concentrating on your imperfections, look to a perfect God who wants to provide for you. When God looks at His children, He sees Jesus' perfect life given up for us. God loves you and will give you everything you need to walk in truth. That is your reality.

Prayer

God, thank You for giving me access to abundant life. Please show me the areas where the enemy has been stealing from me. I do not want to have a thought about myself that You don't have about me. What expectations do I have of myself that are not from You? Help me see how far I've come rather than how far I think I have to go.

Bring it *home*

How would I live if I knew that I was already seen as enough?

_____

_____

_____

_____

_____

God's fruits
are so much better
than anything you
could earn through
performance!

Day *Four*

"How foolish can you be? After starting your new lives in the Spirit, why are you trying to be perfect by your own human effort?"

Galatians 3:3 ESV

Have you ever come across a blackberry bush in the summer? Where I grew up, there were wild blackberry brambles on the nature trail by my house. Early in the season, it was tempting to pick the unripe, small blackberries because they were the only ones available. They were so hard and unbearably sour that they made our mouths pucker. However, if we waited a few weeks into June, the blackberries were plump, juicy, and delectably sweet.

In a way, our lives resemble a blackberry bush. We go through empty seasons and full seasons—seasons of waiting and seasons of action. Don't get impatient with yourself during the times when you only see unripe blackberries. Pursue Jesus, not perfection, and the fruit will follow.

In Galatians 3:3, Paul is telling us that once we become believers, we need to rely on God's power to transform us. Growth will occur naturally when you are connected to God, but it takes time. Jesus didn't just die for you to go to heaven. He also gave you access to the Holy Spirit, who is helping you become more like Christ each and every day.

Trust that God is working in you, and give yourself grace to be in process. A blackberry bush doesn't beg, stress, and strive to produce blackberries. It happens naturally because that is what it was created to do. Similarly, you will become the person God created you to be and do all the wonderful things He created you to do when you choose to walk with and depend on Him day by day. Be patient!

Galatians 5:22-23 says that the fruit of the Spirit is "love, joy, peace, patience, kindness, goodness, faithfulness, gentleness, and self-control." These are fruits that God wants to work into the life of every believer. As you pursue God, you will experience the fruit of the Spirit naturally in your life because His Spirit lives inside of you. As you desire to love Him more than anything, trust Him to bring the results you long for.

God's fruits are so much better than anything you could earn through performance!

Prayer

God, thank You for giving me Your Spirit. Please water the seeds of love, joy, peace, patience, kindness, goodness, faithfulness, gentleness, and self-control in my life. I want the fruit of the Spirit to flourish! I pray for patience as I grow. Keep me from trying to be perfect by my own human effort as I wait for You to transform me day by day.

Bring it *home*

In what situations do I need the fruit of the Spirit in my life?

_____

_____

_____

_____

_____

Trust God and *rest*.

Day *Five*

"Then Jesus said, 'Come to me, all of you who are weary and carry heavy burdens, and I will give you rest. Take my yoke upon you. Let me teach you, because I am humble and gentle at heart, and you will find rest for your souls. For my yoke is easy to bear, and the burden I give you is light.'"

Matthew 11:28-30, NLT

Hopefully you are feeling a little lighter after this week. The weight of perfectionism has been lifted, and there is room to breathe! In the future, when an expectation arises that you feel like you need to meet, ask yourself: Where did this expectation come from: myself, others, or God?

Here's the truth: God does not place heavy expectations on us. Often, we feel the pressure from authority figures in our lives—parents, teachers, coaches, and even pastors—and assume that God piles on the same weight. It's actually quite the opposite! In the verse above, Jesus tells us to give all our cares to Him and He will give us rest. Then He gives us a glimpse into what He wants us to carry—His weight that is easy and light.

Jesus' words here sound calm and peaceful, but the meaning of them was actually quite unthinkable in His day and age. In Jesus' time, the Jews had to follow the law, which included 613 commandments.[2] If they broke a law, they had to offer an animal sacrifice to renew their relationship with God.

Jesus offered the Jewish people freedom from their heavy religious requirements. By living a perfect life and dying on the cross for our sins, Jesus issued a New Covenant: one where we are made perfect by faith in Jesus, not by what we do.

Jesus offers you rest, not religious requirements.

In our performance-based culture, living a restful life that's marked by trusting in God is against the norm. However, it will lead to true peace.

Do you want rest? Are you craving a break from the hustle, bustle, and constant need to achieve? If so, Jesus is waiting for you with open arms. He doesn't expect you to aim for perfection; He just wants you to aim for His presence. Then, He will take care of the rest.

Prayer

God, thank You for being a God that I can relax and be myself around. I am so grateful for what Jesus did on the cross: freeing me from religious requirements and giving me a real relationship with You. Please help me receive Your rest and never take it for granted. I want Your help in letting go of the stress in my life.

Bring it *home*

In what areas of my life do I need to rest and trust God?

_____

_____

_____

_____

_____

(WEEK FOUR)

Let's talk about your *purpose*

Week *Four*
Let's talk about your purpose

(LIE)

MY LIFE DOESN'T MATTER; I HAVE NO PURPOSE.

TRUTH

I AM DRENCHED WITH GOD-GIVEN PURPOSE.

My life has significant meaning. I am drenched with God-given purpose. Every difficulty and every blessing is meant to show me how to depend on Him. He is preparing me now for what I will need in my future walk with Him, which is bright and beautiful.

Day One

"Yes, you ... my personal choice. God who made you has something to say to you; the God who formed you in the womb wants to help you."

(Isaiah 44:1-2, MSG)

We are kicking off our week talking about purpose. And we are coming against ANY lie that wants to tell us that our lives aren't worth living and we have no purpose. Our lives are drenched with purpose from God.

In Isaiah 44, God says that He chose His people, the nation of Israel. And 1 Peter 2:9 reminds us that we, as God's children, are chosen too!

To be chosen doesn't mean that God randomly picked your name from the lottery of life. The word "chosen" actually means that He took His ever-loving time to choose you. It was intentional, thoughtful, and planned. It's the type of choice based on thorough examination. And His choosing wasn't based on anything you've done. God chose to use you flawed and imperfect. And that's just the beginning.

With this choice, this big-picture mindset, God also formed you. When God says He formed you in your mother's womb, He's giving us a word picture of a potter with clay in hand. You weren't mass-produced on the assembly line of humanity. You weren't assembled on an impersonal metal machine, lifeless and void of emotion. You were created. You were formed by the hands of God.

Think about that for a minute. Just as potters have a personal intentionality and intimacy with their clay—from vision to preparation to completion—the same is true in relation to God's mindset towards you. He knew exactly what He was forming when He formed your life. He took care in making you and had your purpose in mind before He ever placed your life on His potter's wheel.

And for a true artist, no one masterpiece is the same. Every piece the potter makes has their unique imprint on it. Your life was particularly crafted by the hands of God. You are one of a kind. So live like it.

Purpose-filled Daughter, you don't have time to lean into the lie that your life is purposeless. Stop looking at who you were in the past and who others say you are. Lean into God and hear what He says you are: perfectly chosen and formed by God. Then muster up some courage and live out the beautifully purpose-soaked life He's intended for you to live!

Prayer

God, I know that Your Word says I'm chosen and formed by You. I am precious in Your sight. You've made me with an amazing purpose in mind: to love You, know You, and make You known to others. Give me a heart and mind to embrace who You have shaped me to be.

Bring it *home*

How does knowing I'm chosen by God bring purpose to my life?

_____

_____

_____

_____

_____

God cares more about who you are *becoming* than what you are *accomplishing* for Him.

Day Two

"'For I know the plans I have for you,' says the Lord. 'They are plans for good and not for disaster to give you a future and a hope.'"

(Jeremiah 29:11, NLT)

Have you ever wondered what God thinks about you? And if He thinks about you, what are His thoughts about your life? I love that the Word of God can bring some clarity to this question we have all asked ourselves.

Purpose-filled Daughter, just as God had plans for His children in the Old Testament—God has plans for you.

The word "plans" used in this passage is so rich. It refers to the designs, intentions, and purposes of God. It refers to God's thoughts towards His people—you included—as well as the plans or intentions arising from these thoughts. The word is also used in reference to the skillful inventions coming from the mind of an artist.

In context, this verse was spoken to a group of people who were fearing for their lives. They were doubting God's goodness and wondering if He really did have their best interests at heart. In the middle of their doubt, God steps in and assures them He loves them, cares for them, and actually has wonderful plans for their peace, hope, and future.

The same holds true for you today. God has plans of peace for you. This doesn't mean on the outside nothing will go wrong; we all know that's impossible. But it does mean on the INSIDE, we don't need to live in constant striving, fear, or worry. We can rest in an assurance that comes from placing our trust in God and His purpose for our lives.

He has a future in store for you. That's significant here, because the people in this passage were wondering if they would live to see tomorrow. Sometimes life just feels like it's too much—and when it does, there's a promise that you can stand on. In God's eyes, He has a destiny and future for you beyond what you see with your eyes. And that future is filled with hope. When we put our trust in Jesus and His Word for our lives, we always have reason to hope. It's not the kind of hope that says "fingers crossed something good might happen." No, this is a hope that has an assurance attached to it. This word "hope" carries with it an expectation for good, not bad.

That is what God has in store for you. So, anytime you are tempted to believe otherwise, stop those thoughts with the Word of God. Bring truth to your present and future. Your life has purpose in the eyes of God, and that purpose with Him is FILLED with hope, goodness, expectation, and peace.

Prayer

God, I believe that You have amazing plans for my life that are hope-filled, destiny-filled, and overflowing in Your peace-filled presence. Help me to trust in Your plans and not my own and to follow You in everything I do.

Bring it *home*

How does knowing that God has plans for my life fill me with hope?

_____

_____

_____

There are no accidents on God's timetable and that *includes your life.*

Day Three

"Who knows if perhaps you were made queen for such a time as this?"

Esther 4:14, NLT

Let's talk about a courageous woman in the Bible named Esther. If you have time to read the book of Esther in its entirety, do it! The book is located in the first half of your Bible right before Job and Psalms. It's a ten-chaptered, ten-course feast of a story. And the feast only becomes richer the deeper you dig in.

The book of Esther is like a classic heroine tale with a miraculous God at its center. It's a story laced with setbacks and courage, poverty and wealth, pain and overwhelming triumph.

You see, purpose-filled Daughter, you may think that in order to have true purpose in life, you have to experience the right upbringing, walk through no hardship, embrace positive thinking at all times—and basically have a cotton-candy, walking-on-sunshine kind of life. But that simply isn't the case.

Esther lived through hardship. She lost both her parents at a young age, was adopted by her uncle, lived in exile away from her homeland, was surrounded by people who didn't even believe in her God, and experienced oppression for her nationality. Sound relatable? Yet in the middle of all this, God used Esther to save an entire nation.

Yeah, she was probably tempted to believe she didn't have a purpose. It would have been easy to simply hide in the palace and live less than what God created her to be—to believe the lie that her life didn't really matter. But God used a spiritual parent in her life to step in and remind her that she was born for "such a time as this."

Today, let me be that spiritual parent and remind you, Daughter, that you were born for such a time as this. There are no accidents on God's timetable—and that includes your life. The people in your life need you. God wants to work in you and through you. In fact, maybe, just maybe, God will use the very things you wish weren't there—the hardship, the opposition, the doubt or fear—as part of your purpose.

You were born for such a time as this.

Prayer

God, I thank You that my life has purpose. I may not see it, I may even doubt it, but today I choose to believe You. Give me eyes to see the purpose You have for my life. And bring God-loving people to surround me and speak Your truth over me. Amen.

Bring it *home*

What kind of hope can I have knowing God has me here for such a time as this?

_____

_____

_____

_____

_____

→ *Today, let me be that spiritual parent and remind you, Daughter, you were born for such a time as this. There are no accidents on God's timetable—and that includes your life. The people in your life need you. God wants to work in you and through you. In fact, maybe, just maybe, God will use the very things you wish weren't there—the hardship, the opposition, the doubt or fear—as part of your purpose. You were born for such a time as this.*

Day *Four*

"Mighty hero, the Lord is with you!"

(Judges 6:12, NLT)

If you think you're the only one who has ever doubted that your life has purpose or value, think again. The Bible is FILLED with people who doubted their purpose, so welcome to the club! There's comfort that comes from knowing you aren't alone in your doubts—but, Daughter, your strength comes from choosing to believe what God says about you and responding in obedience.

Let me tell you about a man who dealt with massive disbelief in God's purpose for him—a man named Gideon. His story is found in Judges 6. Gideon came from one of the weakest tribes in Israel and was one of the youngest in his family. His occupation was that of a lowly farmer, back when owning farmland wasn't the American Dream made popular by Chip and Joanna Gaines. Basically, Gideon was a nobody.

When he wasn't farming, he spent his days hiding from the biggest bullies of his time, the Midianites. Picture the group of people in your school that you try to avoid because they are mean to everyone. Well, these Midianites took it one step further. They stole the harvest from an entire nation, robbing them of the food they worked so hard for and leaving them to starve.

Sound intense? Yeah, it was. Gideon thought so too. That's why when we first hear of him in the Bible, he's hiding. Gideon, the fearful farmer. In reality, that's who he was.

But God steps right into his hiding place and calls him a "mighty hero."

Don't breeze past this part. While Gideon was hiding in intimidation, doubting God and his purpose, God speaks to Gideon. He calls him a "mighty hero"—not a cowardly, chickenhearted, fearful farmer. He doesn't list Gideon's lack of qualifications or point out his disbelief. He loves him and speaks to his identity and purpose. God defines Gideon by His Word alone. And in God's eyes, Gideon was a mighty hero.

I believe God wants to speak to you today: purpose-filled, mighty hero that you are. He wants to step right into your comfort zone of disbelief and change your identity with His truth— reminding you of who He says you are. With Him, you are a mighty, purpose-filled hero.

Prayer

God, today I choose to believe that I am who You say I am. When I'm tempted to doubt, I'll remind myself that with You, I am a mighty hero. You are using my life. You are sending me, and You are defining me by Your Word.

Bring it *home*

In what ways does Gideon's story encourage me?

_____
_____
_____
_____
_____
_____

(YOU ARE)

the light of the world

God, today I choose to value who I am on the inside over what I do. I was made to be a light for You, so transform my character. Let who I am shine for You and let others be drawn to the brightness of You in me.

Day *Five*

"You are the light of the world. A city that is set on a hill cannot be hidden."

Matthew 5:14, NKJV

You are the light of the world. Wow. If we are looking for a significant purpose, I think we just stumbled upon it in the first sermon Jesus ever preached to a large gathering, called the Sermon on the Mount. Notice Jesus doesn't say, "Man, I hope someday that her life will be light for Me." No, He says YOU ARE the light of the world. It's a purpose statement for believers. In fact, this is the same title He gives Himself in John 8:12, when Jesus says, "I am the light of the world."

So what does it mean to be a light for God? The moment we give our lives to God, being a light for Him is a part of our purpose. And it's not just something we do; it's a purpose in relation to who we are on the inside. You need to get this. In regards to purpose, we often think of what we do, our assignment, as our purpose. But who we are matters more to the heart of God.

Our light comes out as love, joy, peace, patience, kindness, goodness, and staying full of faith in God—it's the fruit of living a life fully surrendered to God (Galatians 5). It's not found in how many Instagram followers we have, the brand new Lululemon outfit we got, or the amount of likes we have on TikTok. Light is found in having a little more patience with your mom, choosing to believe the best about your friend, keeping quiet when you really want to gossip. It's trusting God's Word in the situations throughout your day. It's showing kindness to that kid everyone makes fun of at school. It's the practical stuff. Who we are on the inside is where our purpose is formed, and it bubbles over into what we do.

Because in the end, our purpose really isn't just about us. Our lives are meant to draw people to Jesus. Don't get caught up in the trap of chasing a wrongly defined purpose. Stop worrying about what you are supposed to do in the next season, and just let God work on your character as you surrender to Him. That's the brightest light of all.

Hold what you do with open hands and cling to who you are: a beautifully created, purpose-filled daughter of God.

Prayer

God, today I choose to value who I am on the inside over what I do. I was made to be a light for You, so transform my character. Let who I am shine for You and let others be drawn to the brightness of You in me.

Bring it *home*

Does who I am on the inside impact what I do on the outside? Why or why not?

_____

_____

_____

_____

_____

WEEK FIVE

Let's talk about your *relationships*

Week *Five*
Let's talk about your relationships

(LIE)

WHAT OTHERS THINK OF ME DETERMINES MY VALUE.

TRUTH

WHAT GOD SAYS ABOUT ME DETERMINES MY VALUE.

I can't control others, but I can ask the Holy Spirit to help transform me for the better.

Day One

"I'm no longer calling you servants because servants don't understand what their master is thinking and planning. No, I've named you friends because I've let you in on everything I've heard from the Father."

(John 15:15, MSG)

This week, we are silencing the lie that what other people think about us determines our value. So let's go deep as we talk about friendship and community, because surrounding yourself with the right people really makes a difference.

Many times, we allow what others say about us to determine our value because we actually value their opinion more than God's. That's a truth you can reread. But remember, God wants to be your closest friend. Only He should hold the title of BFF in your life.

A relationship with God is what you and I were created for. He is the best friend we could ever ask for. All other relationships are just icing on the cake. And I don't think we can ever be the friends we were meant to be with others until we get our identity and fulfillment from God alone. When God is our best friend, His voice matters more to us than the voices of others. In fact, His voice silences all other voices speaking against our identity in Him.

The more time you spend with any friend, the closer you will get. Get to know God through consistent time with Him. Cultivate a longstanding friendship and intimacy with Him. Talk to Him like you would a friend on the phone. Invite Him into your day. Get to know Him by reading His love letter to you: the Bible.

When our identity takes its cues from our earthly friendships—such as how many friends we have, who likes us, whether or not we make all our friends happy, the number of likes we have on social media, or ensuring that everyone is speaking well of us—it's a recipe for disaster.

We need to stand in confidence in who we are—in Whose we are—before we can cultivate healthy friendships with others.

My friendship with God is the most cherished friendship I have. It can be yours too. Come to Him just as you are. Just be you, the God-created version of you. He loves that version the best. Let God's voice trump all others!

Prayer

God, will You be my best friend? I give all of my life to You. Help me seek You as the first One I go to for advice, the One whose opinion matters most to me. Create in me the desire to value our friendship above all others.

Bring it *home*

How can I cultivate my friendship with God this week?

_____

_____

_____

_____

We all want to find *our people.*

We all desire that deep connection. We want someone to know our deepest parts and to love us anyway. That type of community doesn't just come naturally,

we have to look for it and *fight for it.*

-Jennie Allen

Day Two

"For God is working in you, giving you the desire and the power to do what pleases him."

(Philippians 2:13, NLT)

We've been talking about the fact that what others say about you doesn't determine your worth. But let's look inward for a minute—because many times, the kind of person you are is the kind of person you will attract in life. Now, this isn't always the case. We all know that we can't silence all the haters. Sometimes we don't even do a single thing wrong and still people just don't like us.

We can't change them, but we can ask God to help transform us. For every believer, God promises that He is working on the inside of us. We can ask Him to work on our character to be the kind of person He wants us to attract.

- If you want to have friendships that encourage you in your faith, ask God to help you be a faith-filled person.
- If you want friends who have a personal, intimate relationship with God, develop your intimacy with God through prayer and reading the Bible consistently.
- If you want friendships that are encouraging, ask God to help you encourage others.
- If you want friends who have integrity (doing the right thing when nobody's watching), ask God to help you make the right choices both publicly and privately.

- If you want friends who dream big dreams with God and act as if nothing is impossible with Him, you dream with God first.
- If you want friends who don't gossip behind your back, speak well of others and avoid spreading rumors.
- If you want a friend who is quick to forgive and cover offenses in love, ask God to help you extend forgiveness readily.
- If you want a friend you can have fun with, make fun a priority in life.
- If you want a friend whose identity isn't based on you, then ask God to help you base your identity on Him first.

Many times, you attract who you are—so having great friendships starts with you. Ask God to shape your character behind the scenes to be a good friend to others. Be moldable on the journey.

Prayer

God, would You help me to be a great friend to others? Help me to be the same person in private as I am in front of people and to be the God-loving kind of person I want to attract.

Bring it *home*

What type of friends do I want in my life?

_____

_____

_____

_____

Day Three

"A man who has friends must himself be friendly..."

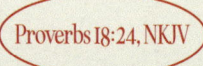

I love that the Bible shares so much wisdom about life, including how to cultivate friendships. I think I'm accurate in my assumption that everyone wants to have supportive friendships surrounding them. But how do they happen? Do you simply wake up one morning and magically have a plethora of friends by your side? Unfortunately, that's not how friendships work.

I see a lot of girls approach friendship like they're being chosen for a dodgeball team. They stand on the sidelines of life, secretly hoping that someday the one person they admire will pick them. Round after round of team selection commences and they are left wondering why no one ever picked them. I've been there.

In Proverbs 18:24, the Bible says that a man who has friends must himself be friendly. In order to receive friendship, you must first extend it.

Don't be shy about it. Start pursuing people you want to be friends with. Surround yourself with girls who love Jesus. If you don't know any girls who love Jesus, find a good church and ask God to place the right girls in your path. Invite them over for a hangout night. Meet up at church every week and attend a church experience together. Go out to a coffee house and get a giant cookie to share. Be generous in a way that matters to them. You can't be friends with someone you don't spend time with, so go the extra mile and start pursuing the godly relationships you desire. I promise it will be well worth the effort. Surrounding yourself with the right people will only help grow your intimacy with Jesus.

And yes, not everyone will accept your invitation. But some will, and then a friendship will be born. Remember, even when your relationships start to blossom, don't stop pursuing.

Prayer

God, would You help me to not only be the right friend, but to pursue the right friendships in my life? I want to be surrounded by girls who will help me grow closer to You. Thank You, God.

Bring it *home*

Is there someone in my life I need to pursue for friendship?

_____

_____

_____

_____

_____

_____

_____

You're gonna be as close as you are *vulnerable* enough to share.

You have to be the one that goes first. Gather some people, and tell them you need community. Tell them some things about yourself. That's the beginning of great, healthy community. It's scary and vulnerable, but it's worth it.

-Jennie Allen

Day *Four*

"Where there is no counsel, the people fall; But in the multitude of counselors there is safety."

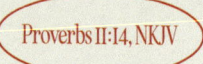

Proverbs 11:14, NKJV

What do we do when our feelings are hurt by other people? I think naturally we want to protect ourselves and hide. I mean, who in their right mind would want to be treated poorly by others?

Think about it: when someone is mean to us at school, we do everything we can to avoid that person because it's awkward. We take the extra-long way around the school to get to third period. We pack our lunch and eat outside or sit at the furthest table in the lunchroom—in the cobwebbed corner where nobody will notice us. We stay in the bathroom stall a little longer than necessary and run with lighting speed straight from our last class to our car—all to avoid a certain someone.

Basically, we want to isolate ourselves in order to protect ourselves. To fly under the radar so no one will notice us. And to our little brains, it makes sense. But the Word of God speaks something different to us. In Proverbs 18:1, the Bible says that a person who isolates himself is unwise. The very thing we want to do to protect ourselves, God calls unwise.

God has a better way, sweet Daughter.

Instead of isolating yourself when you are hurt, try surrounding yourself with the right people. Don't hide away in the shadows carrying your hurt by yourself. Don't brush it off like it's no big deal. Share it with the right people.

Tell a trusted parent or mentor—someone who can allow you to be honest in a non-threatening, trustworthy environment. Give them access to your world. Let them surround you and remind you of what God's Word says in those situations.

Can I be that person for a moment in your life right now? You are so beautifully loved. No matter what others have said about you in the past, remember that they don't deserve the right to determine your value. God loves you. He is for you. He is with you even right now. And I am praying with you that He is going to surround you with the right people who will push you towards full surrender to Him.

You are deeply loved.

Prayer

God, help me not to withdraw when someone hurts me with their words; instead, help me to surround myself with the right people. The people who see me as You see me and remind me of my identity found in Your Word.

Bring it *home*

Why does surrounding myself with the right people matter?

_____
_____
_____
_____
_____

Day *Five*

"Then Peter came to him and asked, 'Lord, how often should I forgive someone who sins against me? Seven times?' 'No, not seven times,' Jesus replied, 'but seventy times seven!'"

Matthew 18:21-22, NLT

Ah, the journey of forgiveness. It's true that some wounds go deeper than others, but forgiveness must be at the core of any lasting friendship. And it must be something you embrace towards everyone, even the people you don't like very much.

When someone says something mean to us, even if we know it's not true, it's really easy to get offended and bitter. We often want to withhold forgiveness so that we can get back at them. But forgiveness is more for your heart than for the person who offended you. Forgiveness is an attribute of God's character that is so important to develop. You see, the one person unforgiveness hurts most is YOU.

Studies have found that forgiveness actually reaps huge benefits on our lives, including improved sleep and reduced levels of pain, anxiety, depression, and stress.[3] Those are some crazy benefits, all from forgiving others. Forgiveness is essential to every healthy relationship because we are all faulty. None of us is perfect. We will make mistakes regularly. Decide ahead of time that you will forgive when the time comes—because it will come.

Now, let me clarify: to forgive someone doesn't mean that what they did to you wasn't wrong. It also doesn't mean that you need to put yourself in an abusive situation. The word "forgiveness" in Greek means to "let go from one's power or one's further notice."[4] Forgiveness means that you are placing your pain into the hands of God and freeing others from any debt they may owe you.

Extending forgiveness is just the first part of the journey; we also need to ask for forgiveness. The humility to admit when you make mistakes is invaluable and shows spiritual maturity.

Readily forgive those around you. Readily ask for forgiveness. Remember, we can't control what others do to us, but—with God's help—we can choose how we will respond. Freely give and freely receive forgiveness, asking God for the help to do it.

Prayer

Father, I'm sorry for the times in life when I say or do something mean to others. When those times come, will You help me to ask for forgiveness? And when others are mean to me, would You help me to quickly forgive?

Bring it *home*

Is there someone in my life I need to extend forgiveness to?

_____

_____

_____

_____

WEEK SIX

Let's talk about *truth*

Week *Six*

Let's talk about truth

EVERYONE HAS THEIR OWN TRUTH.

(TRUTH)

JESUS IS THE WAY THE TRUTH AND THE LIFE.

Day One

"For a time is coming when people will no longer listen to sound and wholesome teaching. They will follow their own desires and will look for teachers who will tell them whatever their itching ears want to hear. They will reject the truth and chase after myths."

(2 Timothy 4:3-4, NLT)

Every year, Oxford Dictionaries picks a word of the year that embodies the spirit of the past 365 days. In 2016, they chose the word "post-truth."[5] It's an adjective that describes when "objective facts are less influential in shaping public opinion than appeals to emotion and personal belief." Since 2016, sociologists have described the times we live in as a post-truth era.

We live in a time where many people reject God's Truth. Instead, everyone has their "own truth" that they can define based on their emotions or personal beliefs. People get "canceled" or even bullied if they aren't 100% accepting of someone else's truth.

The Apostle Paul warned about this in 2 Timothy 4. He prophesied, "For a time is coming when people will no longer listen to sound and wholesome teaching. They will follow their own desires and will look for teachers who will tell them whatever their itching ears want to hear. They will reject the truth and chase after myths."

Perhaps you've felt the effects of this in your school lessons or conversations with your peers. This kind of cultural environment can be confusing and make it hard to know what's real. Here's the thing: when we tolerate the idea that everyone has their own truth, we're putting truth in the hands of humans rather than an all-knowing, all-powerful God. This leads to chaos and confusion.

Thankfully, as daughters of God, we have the Spirit of Truth living inside us to help us know what's true and what's a lie. As Christians, we believe that the only thing that can define truth is the Word of God.

At the end of the day, people want to live by their own truth because they want to validate the way they live, even when it's selfish or harmful to themselves and others. When we try to live our own truth rather than THE truth, we're only living a lie. God offers us access to truth that will set us free and root us in the reality of His love.

Prayer

God, thank You for Your constant truth in a world where it seems like everything is always shifting and changing. Please make me so hungry for Your truth that it makes every lie and false way of living unappetizing. Please give me the courage to stand for truth in love, even when it's difficult.

Bring it *home*

In what areas of my life do I need to stand up for God's truth?

_____

_____

_____

If He's the first place that you go,
you've made Him

the Way

If He's the first place you get your value,
you've made Him

the Truth

If He's the first place you give your best,
you've made Him

the Life

—Charlotte Gambill

"Jesus told him, 'I am the way, the truth, and the life. No one can come to the Father except through me.'" –John 14:6, NLT

Day Two

"Jesus told him, 'I am the way, the truth, and the life. No one can come to the Father except through me.'"

John 14:6, NLT

Have you ever gotten lost before? Whether it's losing your mom in the store as a little kid or getting turned around on a nature walk, getting lost is never a good feeling. Sometimes, we can feel a little lost in life—unsure of where we are going or if everything is going to be okay.

This was exactly how the disciples were feeling before Jesus died on the cross. On the day before He was crucified, Jesus gave His disciples some encouragement on how they could follow Him after He was gone.

Jesus said, "You know the way to where I am going." Thomas, one of the disciples, was confused. He said, "No we don't, Lord. We have no idea where you are going, so how can we know the way?" Jesus told him, "I am the way, the truth, and the life. No one can come to the Father except through me." (John 14:4-6)

Thomas was looking for a map, but Jesus offered him a lifestyle instead. Jesus isn't saying He KNOWS the way, the truth, and the life. He's saying He IS the way, the truth, and life. The Greek word for truth is alētheia, and it means "objectively, what is true in any matter under consideration."[6] In this statement, Jesus makes it clear that there are not multiple truths. Following Jesus is the only way to know God, understand the world we live in, and go to heaven.

Truth is not just an intellectual concept. It should affect the way we live our lives. To do that, truth has to move from our head to our heart. Now, let's be clear—living in truth and following Jesus does not mean that you have to know all the answers. Like Thomas, you may find yourself saying "I have no idea where I'm going, so how can I know the way?" To that, Jesus says, "You don't need to have the answers. Just follow Me."

How do we know how to follow Jesus? First, we have the Word of God. Second, we have the Holy Spirit. In the same conversation, Jesus told His disciples, "If you love me, obey my commandments. And I will ask the Father, and He will give you another Advocate who will never leave you. He is the Holy Spirit, who leads into all truth." (John 14:15-17) You have this Advocate too! When you feel lost and unsure of what's true, the Holy Spirit will show you the way, the truth, and the life.

Prayer

God, thank You for sending Your son, Jesus, and giving me the Holy Spirit so that I am never truly alone or lost. You are the way to the truth, and following Jesus is the only way to experience truth. Give me the boldness to live for You and opportunities to share my faith with others. I love You.

Bring it *home*

How can I fully follow Jesus this week?

_____

_____

_____

_____

The simplicity of faith is this:

Taking God's

—Word for it.
-Jackie Hill Perry

Day Three

"Don't let anyone capture you with empty philosophies and high-sounding nonsense that come from human thinking and from the spiritual powers of this world, rather than from Christ."

(Colossians 2:8, NLT)

Do you ever feel like there are some areas of life where your faith just can't help? Sometimes it is hard to see how Biblical truth can help us with our grades, friendship drama, or boy problems. The world is all too eager to fill in those gaps with advice—and often, it's bad advice.

Daughter, let me encourage you today: God wants to speak truth into every area of your life, from the big-time decisions to the daily details. With God, you have everything you need. The verse above, Colossians 2:8-10, confirms this! We start to recognize God's voice the more time we spend in His Word—and not just one verse here and there. Spend extended time reading large portions of scripture; it will help you discern between lies and the truth.

Colossians 2:10 says that we are complete in Christ. As a daughter of God, you don't need anything else to be whole. Here's what "complete" means according to the original Greek the passage was written in: to cause to abound. To furnish or supply liberally. To render perfect. Fill to the brim, so that nothing shall be wanting to full measure. To cause God's will to be obeyed as it should be, and God's promises to receive fulfillment.[7]

Isn't that incredible?! When Jesus died on the cross and resurrected, He conquered death once and for all! Nothing can come against Him. And as a believer, His Spirit, the Holy Spirit, lives inside you. When you call on the powerful name of Jesus, you bring the Kingdom of Heaven to earth. You can bring the peace, healing, and joy of God into any circumstance.

It's true, there are many voices that come against this truth. Whether it is human ego or spiritual powers, there are very real forces trying to convince you that Jesus is not enough.

This is why knowing the truth is so powerful. When you hold tight to scripture, you can smash down any philosophy or nonsense that does not agree with the Word of God.

Prayer

God, thank You that Your truth is relevant for every aspect of my life. You make me complete, and I want to know the fullness of the power that comes from You. Please show me how to bring the Kingdom of Heaven into my school, home, and friendships. Protect me from holding onto any philosophy or belief that comes from anywhere besides You.

Bring it *home*

Is there an area of my life where I am not believing the truth of God?

_____

_____

_____

_____

_____

If and when we determine the nature of God according to what we go through, we will end up worshiping a God made in our own image.

-Jackie Hill Perry

Day Four

"Trust in the Lord with all your heart; do not depend on your own understanding. Seek his will in all you do, and he will show you which path to take."

Proverbs 3:5-6, NLT

Have you ever done a trust exercise with someone? Here's how it works: with your eyes squeezed shut and your arms crossed on your chest, you fall back into the arms of your partner, completely dependent on them to catch you.

Trusting God works a lot like this: we surrender our control and fall into His arms, believing that He won't let us fall. Trust is defined as the firm belief in the reliability, truth, or strength of someone or something. When we trust in God, we get to exchange our abilities, truth, and strength for His! That's a huge weight off our shoulders!

Scripture encourages us to trust in God even when we don't understand why. At some point, we have to let go of our need to understand and trust that following Jesus, the personification of truth, will lead us to the best outcome.

In the scripture above, we are told to trust God with all our hearts. Trusting God means letting go of our own understanding or the way that we think is correct. Though this is difficult, it's for the best. We don't know what's best for us, but God does.

Remember, many people live by their "own truth" because they want to do what's comfortable or beneficial to them. Our understanding often steers us towards what we want, not God's best for our lives. Our feelings and sin nature will often lead us astray. When you trust God, He will show you the best path to take. However, He rarely shows you where the path leads. Trust leads to more trust!

Daughter, you can trust the truth that's found in the Word of God. It will never lead you astray. Consider: Are there some areas where you need to stop trying to understand and start trusting? The more we move towards faith, the more understanding will come.

Prayer

God, thank You for being so trustworthy. Help me to learn that I can trust You even when I don't always understand what You are doing. Today, I want to fall into Your arms and give You any stress, problems, or questions that I'm carrying. I trust that You are good and that Your plans for me are good. Amen.

Bring it *home*

What are some practical ways I can trust God this week?

_____

_____

_____

_____

_____

God, please make me *so hungry* for your truth that it makes every lie and false way of living unappetizing.

-Hannah Grieser

Day *Five*

"Keep on asking, and you will receive what you ask for. Keep on seeking, and you will find. Keep on knocking, and the door will be opened to you. For everyone who asks, receives. Everyone who seeks, finds. And to everyone who knocks, the door will be opened."

Matthew 7:7-8, NLT

Yesterday, we talked about trusting the truth even when we don't understand it. However, trusting God does not mean that we can't ask questions. There are some seasons where it feels like we are living in a big question mark, unsure of why certain things are happening (or not happening) to us.

Jesus wants us to draw near to Him in those seasons. In Matthew 7, Jesus said, "Keep on asking, and you will receive what you ask for. Keep on seeking, and you will find. Keep on knocking, and the door will be opened to you. For everyone who asks, receives. Everyone who seeks, finds. And to everyone who knocks, the door will be opened."

Asking, seeking, and knocking are ongoing actions. Jesus doesn't want us to just ask one question. He wants us to keep on asking them and seeking the answers from scripture, prayer, and godly community.

There's room for questions in our relationship with God. The pursuit of truth always entails questions, and those questions bring us closer to God. Sometimes, we have to wait months or years before we get an answer to a question or prayer. That's because "asking" is often more about building a relationship with God than it is about getting an answer. God values our questions, but as we keep on looking for truth, God shows us that His presence is better than any answer. When we draw near to Him, He draws near to us.

So keep on asking your questions. They are the keys to building a living, breathing, growing relationship with God. The best feeling in the world is to know that you know God and He knows you!

Prayer

God, forgive me for the times when I think I have it all worked out. I want to come to You for answers before I go to anyone else. Help me to trust You in the journey even when I don't have all the answers.

Bring it *home*

What questions do I have about truth? Write down two questions for God here.

_____
_____
_____
_____
_____
_____

Lie Detector Tests

ASK YOURSELF: "WHO TOLD YOU...?"

Have you ever wondered why you think what you think about yourself? Where did it come from?

After Adam and Eve sinned in Genesis 3, the first question God asks them is, "Who told you…?" This is a great tool to use in regards to your thoughts.

As Christians, it's important to think about what we are thinking about. We need to stop long enough to ask ourselves: Is what I'm thinking about lining up with what God says about me?

Oftentimes, we are rehearsing lies or even partial truths and then clinging to them as absolute truths for our lives. The lies we believe begin to form our identities, purpose, and worth—when only God was meant to hold that role.

So who told you that thing you're thinking about yourself? Was it a friend at school, a random social media post, an angry parent—or is it just your emotions talking?

If it doesn't line up with what God says about you, kick it out and replace it with God's Word.

TEST 2

WHAT DO THE THOUGHTS SOUND LIKE?

Here's a simple way to discern whether the thoughts you are thinking are God's best for you, according to His Word, or a badly built mindset you've crafted along your journey.

The voice of God will sound much different than the other voices that are trying to bring you harm.

Consider:
- God's voice convicts you in love; other voices bring condemnation and guilt.
- God's voice encourages and brings reassurance; other voices bring fear and discouragement.
- God's voice brings clarity and confirmation, even in the unknown; other voices bring confusion.
- God's voice brings peace; other voices bring worry.
- God's voice leads and guides through trust; other voices tend to push and rush us.
- God's voice brings comfort; other voices bring chaos and compromise.[8]

Let's get really practical here. How do we distinguish God's Truth from the lies we believe? Use these simple lie detector tests to guide you toward God's truth for your life.

Few final words

Just because you've finished this book doesn't mean your journey has ended—Your journey with God has just begun.

Remember, your relationship with God is like any other relationship in life. In order to grow the relationship, you need to spend time together. Give God the best of who you are and I promise He won't disappoint. Dive into His Word and discover a million promises that are yours for the taking. Your purpose in God is too great for you to live with anything less than all-in devotion to God.

And know today, sweet daughter, that you are not unlovable, forsaken, or unworthy. You are found, loved, and known by God. You are beautiful and perfectly chosen. You may not see it now, but this is your reality. Stop believing the lies. Start believing the truth of God. Let go of what once was. Embrace what is. Pursue His Truth and remember: you are never alone.

There are people on this end of the story who are praying for you and see with God-given perspective the beautiful creation that you are and will become. We are championing God's best in you. We love you. We are here for you. We are cheering you on in your faith-walk with God. Praying that your identity becomes so secure in Him and the truth of His Word, that you will stand strong, courageous, and grounded in Christ—no matter what comes your way.

Remember who you are, Choose Truth, and let God alone define you—God-confident daughter that you are.

Salvation Prayer

I couldn't end this book without giving you the opportunity to pray and commit your life to Jesus. My prayer is that you have seen His love for you woven intricately throughout these pages and that you have felt His desire for you specifically in every chapter. Having a relationship with Jesus is the best decision you could ever make. The Bible says in Romans 10:9-10 that if we confess with our mouth that Jesus is Lord and believe in our heart God raised Him from the dead, we will be saved. Join me in the following prayer of asking Jesus to be Lord of our lives.

Jesus, I admit my need for You. I believe that You are God, that You died on the cross for my sins and rose again. I invite You to be Lord of my life. I surrender to You my hopes, my dreams, my hurts, and my wounds. All that I am I lay at Your feet. Take control of my life and make something beautiful. In Jesus name, amen.

Whether you have prayed that prayer for the first time or the tenth time, I am celebrating with you today. Start reading your Bible and praying daily. Get to know God, approach Him like you would any other friendship in your life. Spend time with Him. Find a great church and surround yourself with other people that can bring out God's best in you. The journey has just begun ...

About Jamie
Author

Jamie Klusacek is an author and speaker who lives in Colorado with her amazing Czech-born husband, Milan, and four gorgeous daughters, Grace, Anna, Selah, and Noella. Her primary passion is to love God and love people—to walk courageously obedient with Jesus and help others do the same. She believes that God is near and still speaks personally to us today. Each of our lives is marked for miracles as we join in this adventure to make His name known throughout the earth.

Whether serving at her church, drinking steaming hot tea and writing books, singing bedtime lullabies to her children, or baking chocolate chip cookies with friends—Jamie believes that each day is a gift to be cherished, holding opportunities for us to share the genuineness of God's love with those around us. She would love to hear from you.

Connect with Jamie

jamieklusacek.com

◉ @jamieklusacek

About Hannah
Co-Author

Ever since Hannah could hold a pencil, she has loved writing and hearing people's stories. Currently, she serves as the content director at a faith-based financial education nonprofit and pursues freelance work on the side. Hannah is passionate about spreading truth through the written word and has ghostwritten three books and several devotionals. In her free time, Hannah enjoys spending time with her husband Mason and dog Gabe, cooking, and doing pretty much anything in the sunshine.

Connect with Hannah

www.milkandhoneyco.org
For writing inquiries, contact
hannahgrieserwriting@gmail.com

Acknowledgments

I would love to say thank you first and foremost to Jesus. Without Him, none of this would be possible. You are our Truth.

For Hannah Grieser, co-author, who wrote two of the most memorable chapters in this book. Who jumped on board, with enthusiasm, inspiration, and Biblical truth, so that we could write this book for precious daughters we don't even know.

Tiffany and Autumn and the THERE{4} Gathering who championed the book from dream to reality. For their prayers, conversations, and passion to make God's Word known. For their heart to see girls impacted by the love of God and Truth of His Word. This partnership has blown my mind from the beginning.

To our strategic partners, we are in awe of your support and generosity. This project wouldn't be possible without you.

For the teen girls who shared openly and honestly about the lies they sometimes believe and how they need God's Truth in their lives. Your openness and vulnerability was a roadmap for each chapter.

For Bonnie and Suzanne who did the impossible in the editing world and rallied behind the book in record time.

To my husband, Milan Klusacek, who with the help of God walked through the miraculous once again. You said yes—and designed a book within a timeframe that was improbable. My heart is so thankful. The design is breathtaking.

Lastly, to our four girls. Being a mom of three teenagers has given me a front row seat to what you face daily in your season of life—and you are so courageous. Thank you for your honesty, openness, and love. You make me realize what a blessing it is to be your mom every day. I thank God for you. This book is for you.

Photography

All photos provided by *pexels.com* unless otherwise noted. Photographers, you continue to inspire me.

Intro Pages
Flowers: Leeloo TheFirst
Girls: Aline Viana Prado

Week One
Mirror: Nadine Wuchenauer
Door: Mitchell Lou
Flower: Evie Shaffer

Week Two
Flower Girl: Marta Dzedyshko
Petals: Sapphire Alsh
Peonies: Leeloo TheFirst
Girls: Aline Viana Prado
Red Flowers: Irina Iriser

Week Three
Mirror: Yuliia Tretynychenko
Girls: Polina Tankilevitch
Pineapple: Karolina Grabowska
Girl: Cottonbro Studio

Week Four
Van: Gya Den
Window Girl: Furknsaglam
Roses: Isabelle Taylor
Girl: Leeloo TheFirst
Queen: Bestbe Models

Week Five
Girls on Car: Elijah O'Donnell
Three Girls: Pavel Danilyuk
Besties: Anna Tarazevich
Shoes: Bianca Gasparoto

Week Six
Roses: Irina Iriser
Book: Wendy van Zyl
Girl: Matheus Natan
Truck: Tuur Tisseghem
Flowers: Anthony Đ

Ending Pages
Girl with Purse: Monica Turlui
Pink Flowers: Leeloo TheFirst
Window: Jeffrey Czum
Camera Girl: Jack Redgate

Footnotes

For your study time: Our Hebrew and Greek word definitions and references are found in the Hebrew-Greek Key Word Study Bible, AMG Publishers.

[1] Psychologytoday.com, How Many Decisions do we Make Each Day
[2] Jewfaq.org, 613 Commandments
[3] hopkinsmedicine.org
[4] Hebrew Greek Study Bible, Matthew 6:12
[5] Languages.oup.com, Word of the Year 2016
[6] Greek Word, 225, Hebrew Greek Study Bible
[7] Blueletterbible.org
[8] Drmichellebengtson.com, Hearing God's Voice